discovermore

Learning Social Studies Skills

Exploring Voices from History

Marie Harts

Britannica Educational Publishing

IN ASSOCIATION WITH

THE ROSEN PUBLISHING GROUP

Published in 2025 by The Rosen Publishing Group, Inc.
2544 Clinton Street, Buffalo, NY 14224

Editor: Shannon Harts
Book Design: Michael Flynn

Photo Credits: Cover Prostock-studio/Shutterstock.com; (series background) Dai Yim/Shutterstock.com; p. 5 (top) https://commons.wikimedia.org/wiki/File:Chino_Garcia_Oral_History_and_Screening_of_CHARAS_is_Alive_on_Spaceship_Earth_(40301839990).jpg; pp. 5, 20 (bottom) courtesy of the Library of Congress; pp. 6, 18 LightField Studios/Shutterstock.com; p. 7 soumen82hazra/Shutterstock.com; p. 8 wellphoto/Shutterstock.com; p. 9 Gorodenkoff/Shutterstock.com; p. 11 (top) https://commons.wikimedia.org/wiki/File:Amelia_Earhart_-_GPN-2002-000211.jpg; p. 11 (bottom) Cvandyke/Shutterstock.com; p. 12 sianstock/Shutterstock.com; p. 13 Gilles Paire/Shutterstock.com; p. 14 https://commons.wikimedia.org/wiki/File:Bernardino_de_Sahag%C3%BAn.jpg; p. 15 a40757/Shutterstock.com; p. 16 https://commons.wikimedia.org/wiki/File:Ralph_Ellison_photo_portrait_seated.jpg; p. 17 Jacob Lund/Shutterstock.com; p. 19 McLittle Stock/Shutterstock.com; p. 21 irin-k/Shutterstock.com; p. 22 LEY.corner/Shutterstock.com; p. 23 Antonio Guillem/Shutterstock.com; p. 24 insta_photos/Shutterstock.com; p. 25 Azure Alpine Artistry/Shutterstock.com; p. 26 antoniodiaz/Shutterstock.com; p. 27 Kate Aedon/Shutterstock.com; p. 28 Ground Picture/Shutterstock.com; p. 29 Halfpoint/Shutterstock.com.

Cataloging-in-Publication Data

Names: Harts, Marie.
Title: Exploring voices from history / Marie Harts.
Description: New York : Britannica Educational Publishing, in Association with Rosen Educational Services, 2025. | Series: Discover more: learning social studies skills | Includes glossary and index.
Identifiers: ISBN 9781641901505 (library bound) | ISBN 9781641901499 (pbk) | ISBN 9781641901512 (ebook)
Subjects: LCSH: Oral history--Juvenile literature. | Historians--Juvenile literature.
Classification: LCC D16.14 H347 2025 | DDC 907.2--dc23

Manufactured in the United States of America

Some of the images in this book illustrate individuals who are models. The depictions do not imply actual situations or events.

CPSIA Compliance Information: Batch #CSBRIT25. For further information contact Rosen Publishing at 1-800-237-9932.

Contents

Unwritten History

You might be familiar with reading about history in books, but for some time periods and events, nothing has ever been written down. How can you learn about what happened? Scientists often study artifacts, but artifacts don't usually tell the whole story. What if there is a lot written about a time or event, but not about certain groups? Such groups can include common people, servants, slaves, those in poverty, **minorities**, and women. What kind of history do they have?

All groups of people have personal stories, memories, myths, beliefs, and more. But their history may not be written down. Instead, it may be in spoken words: tales told around campfires, at ceremonies, and at other events. This knowledge is passed down through the generations. It becomes oral, or spoken, history, and a way to learn information, or facts, about the past. Oral history is a study and way of collecting, understanding, and keeping safe a communities' voices and memories.

Many communities have oral history projects. This picture is from an oral history project that was created to collect and keep safe memories of New York City's East Village.

Storytelling, as shown in this picture, is part of oral history. However, while storytelling usually involves simply telling stories, oral history often involves keeping these stories safe for future generations to learn.

WORD WISE

A MINORITY IS A GROUP OF PEOPLE WHO ARE DIFFERENT, SUCH AS IN RACE OR FAITH, FROM THE MORE POPULOUS GROUP OF PEOPLE IN AN AREA OR REGION. POPULOUS MEANS HAVING A HIGH POPULATION, OR NUMBER OF PEOPLE LIVING IN AN AREA.

Types of Oral History

Oral history can take many different forms. It can be an "official" account of the past, passed down by people in charge of keeping **traditions**. Or it can be less formal. What about the stories grandparents tell about the old days? Those are a type of oral history too.

Oral storytelling, a form of oral history, includes voice and gestures. Gestures are body movements, often of the hands, arms, head, or face that are used to show certain feelings or ideas.

WORD WISE

A TRADITION IS A LONG-PRACTICED CUSTOM.

Chants, rhymes, and songs are all forms of oral storytelling.

Oral history can be passed from one person to another by storytellers or singers of tales. These spoken stories may have been shared over hundreds of years. Oral history was common in the past, and it still happens today. Think about a story you told someone recently. Maybe you told your friend about something funny you saw on TV. It can be hard to remember certain details, or small parts, of short, informal stories like these, so they might not be the most reliable, or trustworthy.

Herodotus and Honest History

Herodotus was an ancient Greek writer. Many consider him to be the creator of history as we know it today. He wrote about the people, customs, and events of his day, in the 400s BCE. He learned about those things by talking to people and listening to oral history. He developed a formula, or method, for judging sources of information. The most truthful information is what you have seen for yourself. For instance, if you met the president, you would know what did or did not happen during the meeting. The next best source is what others have told you—through oral history, for example.

A primary source is a newspaper article or interview that provides a firsthand account of an event by someone who saw or experienced it. An interview is a form of oral history.

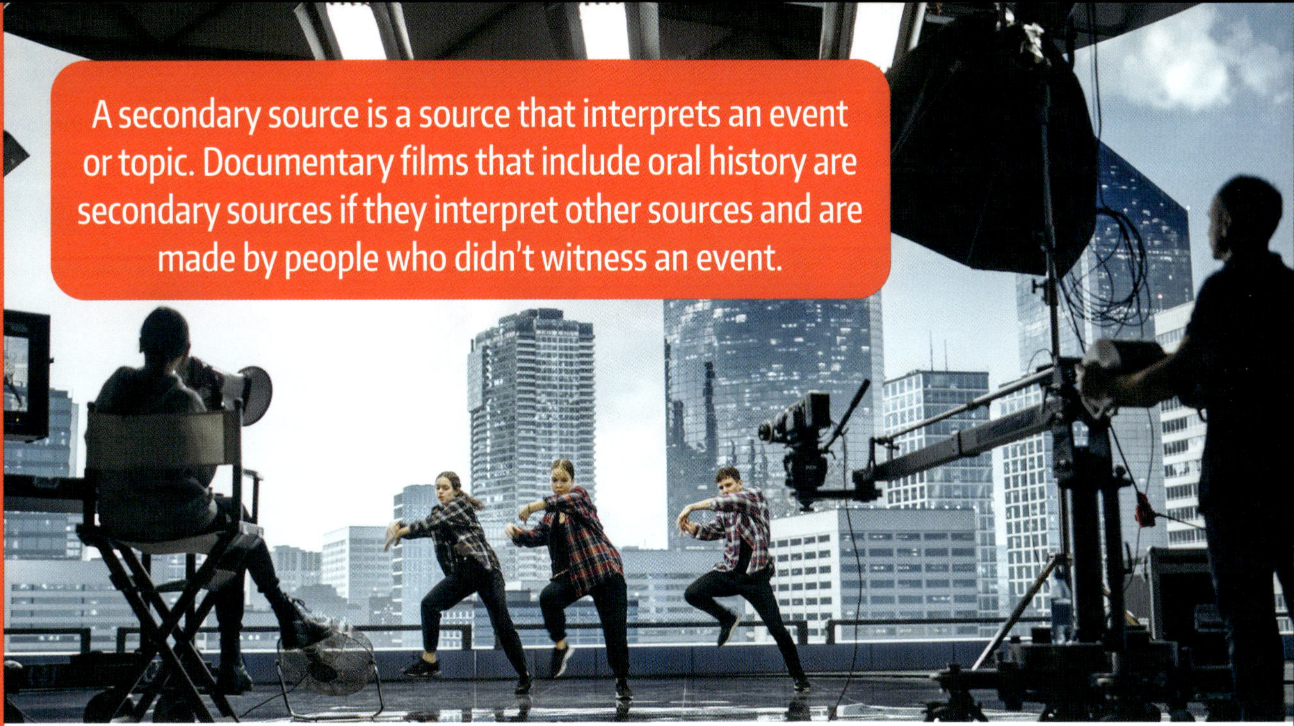

A secondary source is a source that interprets an event or topic. Documentary films that include oral history are secondary sources if they interpret other sources and are made by people who didn't witness an event.

Oral history can be a good primary source. But it also can have problems. Storytellers can add opinions about events they saw. Because you didn't see the events for yourself, you may not be certain about the truthfulness of the story. One way to find out the truthfulness of an oral history is to double check it with other primary sources and with secondary sources.

Consider This

An oral history doesn't usually offer a complete and entirely factual account of a topic or event—it only shows the opinion of a person giving a spoken account. Do you think speaking to people of different opinions for an oral history project can make it more reliable?

Why Oral History Is Important

Oral history usually isn't considered objective. This means it is based on one's personal experiences and emotions rather than facts. For this reason, some historians claim that oral history is not as valuable as other information. However, oral historians think that personal points of view add strength to history. Italian oral historian Alessandro Portelli says that oral sources "tell us not just what people did, but what they intended [wanted] to do, what they believed they were doing, and what they now think they did."

The spoken word can communicate feelings and emotions in ways that the written word cannot. It also can be part of a record of local dialects and accents. One oral history project in England involved studying how the English language has changed over the last 50 years.

A speech by Amelia Earhart is an example of content found in the Library of Congress's Center of Applied Linguistics Collection which aims to document North American English dialects.

compare and contrast

A dialect is a regional variety of a language, differing from the standard language. An accent is a way people in a certain country or region pronounce words. How do you think accents and dialects can tell you similar and different information about an oral history project?

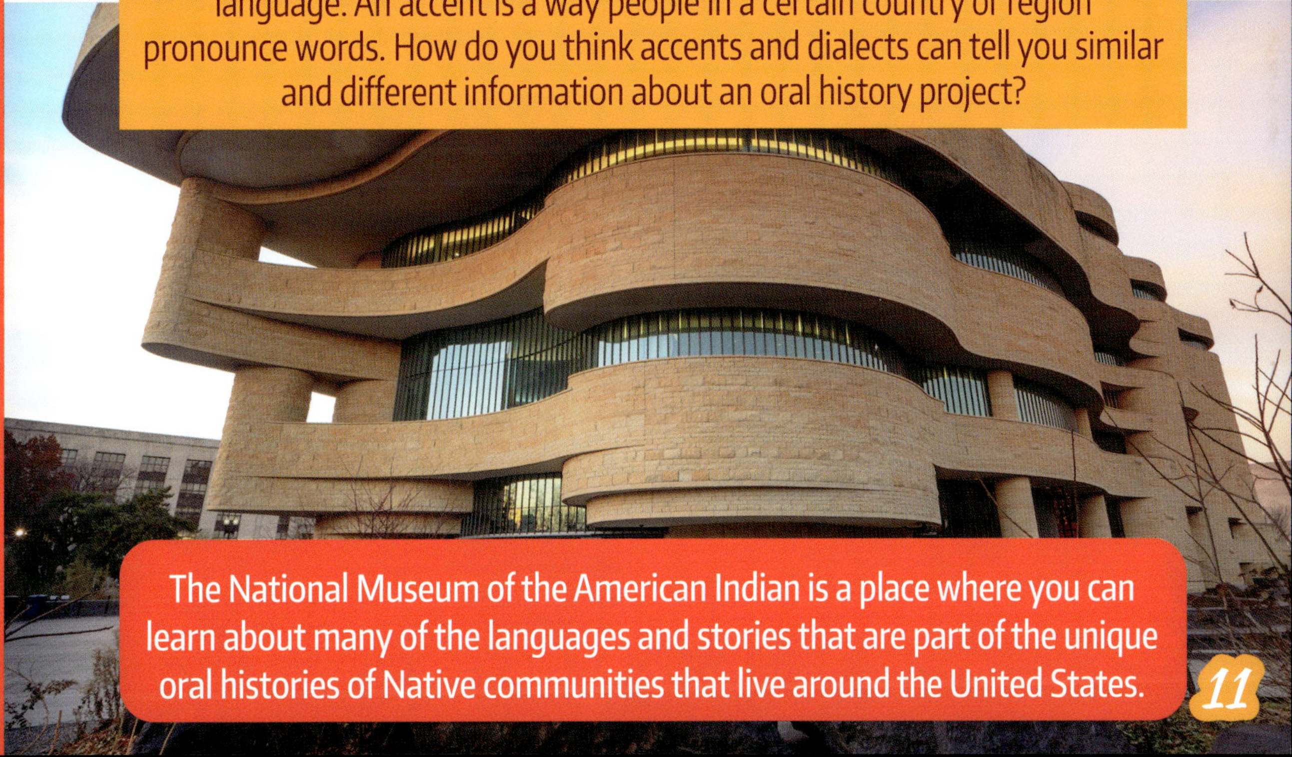

The National Museum of the American Indian is a place where you can learn about many of the languages and stories that are part of the unique oral histories of Native communities that live around the United States.

How Oral History Began

It's believed oral history began in China around 3,000 years ago. Scribes from the Zhou dynasty collected people's sayings for the royal historians to use. During the 400s BCE, the Greek historian Thucydides talked to many eyewitnesses when he wrote about the Peloponnesian War. He checked their reports as well as he could.

This statue of the Greek historian Thucydides is found in Vienna. Thucydides's written account of the Peloponnesian War between Athens and Sparta isn't a form of oral history, but he used oral history interviews to write this piece.

Griots often play instruments when telling their stories. These instruments could include a drum made from the wood of the tamarind tree, a kora that is similar to a harp, and a balafon, which is a type of xylophone.

In the 700s CE, a faith leader named Bede wrote a history of the English people. He wrote that he relied on "countless faithful witnesses who either know or remember the facts."

The Mali Empire ruled in West Africa from the 1200s to the 1500s. It had griots (*gree-oh*) who served as storytellers, singers, and reciters of history, family lines, and traditions. Griots came from certain families, who **preserved** the knowledge of their people. In the region of western and north-central Africa called the Sahel, griots still pass on famous tales mainly through storytelling.

WORD WISE

TO PRESERVE IS TO KEEP SOMETHING SAFE FROM HARM, OR IN ITS ORIGINAL STATE OR CONDITION.

Bernardino de Sahagún, a Spanish **priest**, was another early collector of oral histories. In 1529, he sailed from Spain to Mexico. Once in Mexico, he learned the Aztec language. He talked to Aztec elders who had seen the Spanish conquer their land, and he wrote down their experiences. The best copy of Sahagún's work is known as the *Florentine Codex.*

In the United States, President Abraham Lincoln was killed in 1865. Afterward, his secretary and law partner gathered people's memories about the president. Some information came from interviews with people who had known and worked with Lincoln. These interviews are examples of oral history.

Bernardino de Sahagún's *Florentine Codex* includes 20 songs to gods that Aztecs sang.

A phonograph is an instrument that plays sound recorded on a wax cylinder or grooved disk.

A few decades later, in the 1890s and early 1900s, government researchers recorded thousands of Native American stories and songs on wax cylinders. These cylinders could be played on phonographs. Wax cylinder recordings are now available online through the work of the Cylinder Audio Archive at the University of California, Santa Barbara.

Consider This

Do you think oral histories are more reliable when they are recorded as sound or written down?

WORD WISE

A PRIEST IS A PERSON WHO HAS THE AUTHORITY TO PERFORM OR GUIDE CEREMONIES IN CERTAIN RELIGIONS, OR FAITHS, INCLUDING CHRISTIAN RELIGIONS.

During the Great Depression of the 1930s, the United States government created jobs by hiring people to be interviewers for the Federal Writers' Project. This project involved 300 workers from 24 states writing down the life histories of thousands living in the United States. The interviewers were paid about $20 a week to transcribe, or write down, interviews with everyday Americans. These Americans spoke about life in the past. They also described how they were coping with the hardships of the Great Depression. Some of the best-known stories are the "slave narratives," told by people who had been enslaved in the South. Most of these records are kept in the Library of Congress.

Ralph Ellison was one of the interviewers for the Federal Writers' Project. He later became famous for writing the book *Invisible Man* in 1952.

Podcasts are radio-like programs downloaded and listened to over the internet. They started growing in popularity after the iPod was invented in 2001 and there was a way for people to digitally share audio recordings.

In more recent times, oral histories have been shared in courts, in government **committees**, at educational events, at religious gatherings, and at public meetings. You can often find recordings of these oral histories on TV, websites, or as part of podcast episodes.

WORD WISE

A COMMITTEE IS A GROUP OF PEOPLE PICKED TO DO A CERTAIN JOB OR TO MAKE DECISIONS.

Oral History Today

As in the past, interviews are an important way of collecting oral histories today. Journalists also rely on oral interviews to create news stories. But journalists do not share everything said in an interview. Instead, they usually write about the important information they collect. By contrast, oral histories speak for themselves.

A journalist is someone whose job is to collect, write, and edit news stories for television, magazines, newspapers, radio, and online news sources.

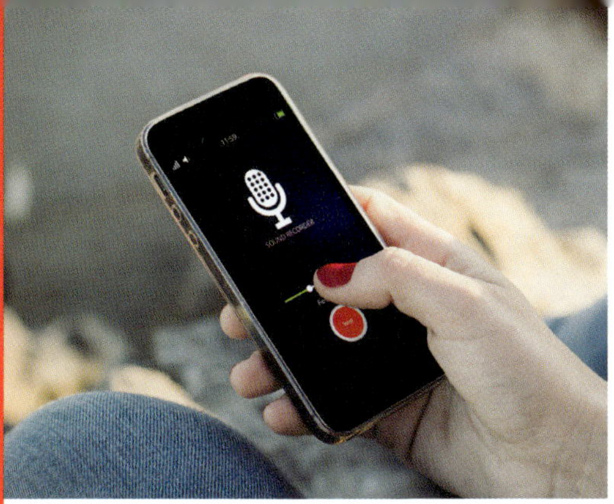

Even if a journalist is working on a written article, they will often record interviews to make sure their reporting is as complete and accurate, or factual, as possible. When recording, journalists are collecting oral history.

The practice of taping interviews to preserve oral history began with the work of U.S. historian Allan Nevins. Starting in 1948, he recorded the memories of many people involved in historical events. He hoped that these recordings would help historians in the future. They also might provide details not found in written records. The goal was to make history as factual as possible. Nevins thought that history should rely on recorded facts more than opinions.

Also in 1948, Nevins founded the Columbia Oral History Research Office. In the beginning, Nevins and other historians only interviewed leaders in fields such as government and business. However, in the 1960s and 1970s, it became more common to interview everyday people.

Consider This

Why do you think morally, and often legally, it is important to ask someone for their okay before recording them?

Oral History and Collective Trauma

Collective **trauma** is the inward distress that a large group of people, often an entire community or culture, experiences in response to a traumatic event. One example of an event that caused collective trauma is the terrorist attacks that happened in the United States on September 11, 2001 and killed about 3,000 people. Several buildings and aircraft were also destroyed. Sadness and anger consumed the nation's people. Soon afterward, citizens began to collect oral histories about the event.

The Library of Congress's September 11, 2001 Documentary Project includes 200 online audio and video interviews, in addition to 45 visual elements, such as this picture of a flight attendant.

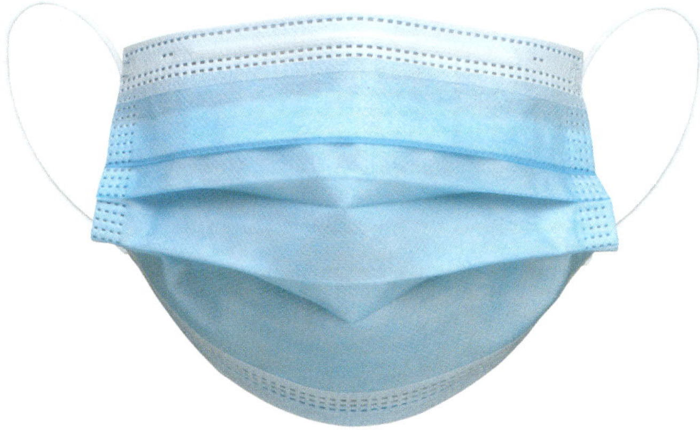

When collecting information from oral interviews during the COVID-19 pandemic, people often wore masks to prevent spreading the deadly COVID-19 sickness.

Columbia University started the September 11, 2001, Oral History Project. Project members interviewed firefighters, police, survivors, and family members of those who died. The 9/11 Memorial & Museum located in New York City maintains a collection of interviews too.

The COVID-19 pandemic is another collective trauma that affected the global community. In 2023, the Library of Congress started the COVID-19 American History Project to collect the oral histories of those affected by the pandemic. A pandemic is a sickness that quickly spreads over a large area, such as the world.

WORD WISE

TRAUMA IS A VERY CHALLENGING AND UNPLEASANT EXPERIENCE THAT CAN CAUSE LONG-LASTING EMOTIONAL AND MENTAL PAIN.

Tech for Collecting Oral History

The technology journalists and historians use to collect oral histories has changed a lot over the years. After wax cylinders came albums and eight-track players. Cassettes and videotapes followed. Then compact discs and DVDs arrived. Today, digital recorders store video and audio in computer files. Many oral historians also now use smartphones to record interviews.

The first digital recorders became available in the late 1970s. Digital recorders are still often used today to record oral histories. However, they have changed to allow interviewers to create digital audio files of interviews.

Cell phones and social media are giving people the tools to easily create and share their own oral histories.

Widespread technology has made it easier than ever to record oral history. Consider the 2008 election of Barack Obama as the 44th president of the United States. His many speeches, interviews, and appearances mean that there is plenty of oral history about him. The challenge for historians is to make meaning from all this information. The University of Virginia Miller Center on Public Affairs has an oral history program that centers on past presidents. The project allows anyone with access to the internet to explore interviews with past presidents and the people who knew and worked with them.

Consider This

How do you think social media has changed the way oral history is collected and shared?

Tips for Interviewing

Most interviews for collecting oral history follow a certain structure. First, the topic must be important enough to preserve for the future. Then the interview should be recorded with audio or video technology. It's important to choose the topic with care. Narrow it down to one event, time, or idea. Examples include a certain job or group of people. Above all, the topic must be specific, or presented clearly and exactly.

When doing research before an interview for an oral history project, one way to tell if a website is trustworthy is to check if it has a page with contact information.

Oral history interviews can be done with nearly anyone around the world thanks to internet video calling programs such as Zoom! However, the quality of the recordings is often not as high as when using other recording tools.

Once you have an idea, you need to learn about it so that you can ask good interview questions. Let's say you decide to interview your grandfather, who spent time as a cowboy in Texas when he was a young man. You would need to learn something about a cowboy's job. You could learn this information from a library or Google search. However, it's important to make sure you only use trustworthy sources!

Consider This

One way to tell if a website is credible is to check if its URL ends in .edu, .gov, or .org. That often means the site was created by a government, educational, or other trustworthy organization. What do you think are some signs a website isn't trustworthy?

After you have researched a topic for your oral history project and interview, it's time to brainstorm some interview questions. Open-ended questions that do not have easy yes or no answers are the best. They provide the most information. For instance, you could ask: Why did you choose to work as a cowboy? How did you find your first job? What surprised you about the work?

Active listening has many nonverbal elements, such as keeping eye contact with an interviewee.

When interviewing someone, it is important to avoid distractions such as pets, small children, and cell phones.

You may have to ask for details. A good way to do that is to use words like “describe” or “explain.” To be sure you understand, you can repeat what you hear in your own words. Then your subject can explain further, if needed. It is important to be patient during interviews, since the person may need to think about the answers. Most important of all is to listen to what the subject says. Active listening is an interviewing skill that involves paying careful attention to what someone is saying, showing you are listening, giving feedback, avoiding judgement, and responding in a respectful way.

Consider This

Do you think it is important to practice active listening skills? Why or why not?

Become an Oral Historian!

Today, you can create and share oral history anywhere using a cell phone app! This app was created by the organization StoryCorps. Its mission is to record and preserve the stories of Americans of different backgrounds and beliefs. Most interviews are 40 minutes long, but interviews can be shorter. More than 400,000 have been completed! When finished, interviews can be heard on the StoryCorps website, archive.storycorps.org.

Asking friends, neighbors, and family members can be the best way to find someone to interview for an oral history project.

While you can practice a little for an oral history interview, it is more important to be yourself and to let the interview flow naturally.

Now it's your turn. Whom would you like to interview? If you think about it, you probably know someone who would like to talk to you. Perhaps that person is a family member or a neighbor. Preparing for the interview will take some work. You'll need questions to ask, a place to sit, and a way to record and save your subject's stories. But the work will be worth it. You will be an oral historian capturing a voice that shapes our understanding of history.

Consider This

It has been said that oral history is different from other forms of history because it tells people less about a historical event, and more about the event's meaning. Why do you think that is?

Glossary

artifact Usually a simple object that shows human work.
ceremony An event to honor or celebrate something.
communicate To share thoughts or feelings by sound, movement, or writing.
culture The beliefs and ways of life of a group of people.
custom An action or way of acting that is commonly or traditionally practiced among a certain group of people.
documentary A movie or TV program presenting factual information about a topic.
future Existing or happening at a later time.
generation A group of individuals born about the same time.
Great Depression A worldwide downturn in the economy that lasted from 1929 through the 1930s.
interpret To explain the meaning of something.
myth A story that was told by a people to explain a practice, belief, or natural event.
poverty Lack of money or possessions.
reciter A person who tells what happened.
scribe A public secretary or clerk, or one who copies manuscripts.
technology Using science, engineering, and other industries to invent useful tools or to solve problems. Also a machine, piece of equipment, or method created by technology.
wax cylinder A device used to record sounds in the 1800s and early 1900s.

For More Information

Books

Boswell, Kelly. *Research Primary Source Audio: Speeches, Oral Histories, Music and More.* North Mankato, MN: Pebble, 2019.

Gregson, Agatha. *Oral Histories.* New York, NY: Gareth Stevens Publishing, 2020.

Websites

Art of Storytelling: Robert Lewis (Cherokee Nation)
youtube.com/watch?v=1c5RqUsT4KQ
This video features a member of the Cherokee Nation sharing a traditional Cherokee story. It is from the Smithsonian National Museum of the American Indian.

Storytelling
kids.britannica.com/kids/article/storytelling/353818
Oral history is part of storytelling. Learn more about storytelling here.

Index